First Letter

of

My Alphabet

Lance Strate

NeoPoiesis Press, LLC

2775 Harbor Ave SW, Suite D, Seattle, WA 98126-2138
Inquiries: Info@NeoPoiesisPress.com
NeoPoiesisPress.com

Lance Strate – First Letter of My Alphabet
ISBN 979-8-9858336-4-5 (pbk)

1. Poetry. I. Strate, Lance. II. First Letter of My Alphabet

Library of Congress Control Number: 2023944329

First Edition

Cover Design: Dale Winslow and Stephen Roxborough

Printed in the United States of America.

For Adas Emuno

Contents

Callings

Wilderness

Words

Beginnings

The Sound of God

one day when I was very young
I was whipping around my little blanket
back and forth through the air
so that it made a sound
and I wondered
is that God?

and I asked my mother
is that God?
am I hitting God?

after all I was told that
God is invisible
and that
God is always there

is that God?
No?
Then tell me
what is God?

I guess my parents didn't know how to answer
so they bought me a book
a children's book of bible stories

it must have been a Christian Old Testament
because it had a picture of God
as an old man with a long white beard
wearing a toga
up in the clouds
God as Zeus

I was fascinated by that image
but I knew that wasn't God

my parents joined Temple Isaiah
a Reform congregation in Forest Hills
now long gone
merged together with other synagogues

Reform Judaism was new to them
but they liked the relaxed attitude
not so many rules you had to follow
it was modern and rational
a product of the Enlightenment
no one told you what to do
just make up your own mind
as an individual

over the entrance of synagogue
chiseled into the stone
were the words of the prophet Micah:

> *What doth the Lord require of thee?*
> *Only to do justly*
> *Love mercy*
> *And walk humbly with thy God*

on Sundays I went to religious school
two hours of stories from the bible
history and literature
and learning about holidays
ethics and philosophy
and singing
and learning prayers
which was mostly singing

I loved it

twice a week
after school
I went to Hebrew School

it was okay
but mostly rote memorization
learning the language and letters

after my father died
the Temple was very good to us
and a place to find comfort

one year they gave me a scholarship
for sleep away camp
a Jewish camp up in the Berkshires

on Friday nights and Saturday mornings
we dressed all in white
t-shirts and white shorts or jeans
and as long as it wasn't raining
we celebrated Shabbat outside
services held in an outdoor sanctuary
surrounded by trees
the sky above us
song leaders playing guitars
ancient prayers sung to new melodies
as folk songs
sometimes with the rhythm
of rock and roll

and sometimes as we prayed
the wind would blow through
the leaves of the trees
making a rustling sound
so beautiful it gave me chills
and there it was

there it was

there it was

the sound of God

The Womb of God

in the womb of God
floating in God's womb
immersed in deepest darkness
seeing only points of light
through eyes closed to the outer world
momentary flashes
so small against the sphere
of constant night
comforted
by rhythms softly sounded
by familiar tones so still and clear
surrounded by the viscous warmth
carried through the currents smooth
rocked back and forth by gentle waves
enclosed within the sacred belly
growing inside the womb of God
expanding and evolving
heaven and earth
and me and you
Creation whole
and complete
in the womb of God

In the Beginning

Sound
a single tear
drops down to the still clear water
a tear into a seamless surface
a rip that opens time
the slightest perturbation
becomes the faintest of vibrations
a ripple of reverberation
through silent mother ocean
a single point without dimension
expanding beyond all comprehension

a touch   the barest brush   a quiver
a note   the slightest fraction of a quaver
a voice   within the vacuum whispers
a song   moves through the void and chaos
in circles   spirals   spheres resounds

Resonance
    bringing reason   order   and distinction
Rhythm
    bringing rhyme and emotion
Melody
    bringing memory and mind
Harmony
    bringing humanity
Counterpoint
    bringing community

a song
a voice
a word
we are the ever-evolving echoes
of the majesty
of the music
of the heavens

Autopoiesis

I did not write this poem
this poem wrote itself
the pen moved of its own accord
across the blue lines   upon the page
scribbling sounds to resonate
within that vast echo-chamber:

The skull, the mind's auditorium

I did not write this poem
it was those who came before:
ancestors of body, mind, and spirit
writing automatically
bards composing dramatically
rhapsodes reciting mimetically
singers singing tales mnemonically
dancers following footsteps of forerunners
priests reenacting rituals of origins and archetypes
primal gestures   music of the hands
primal howls and wails and whispers
primal rhythms beating steadily
primal voice and urge   enlightened
primal bang of drum   explosive
orgasmic   organizing all on its own

    gestating   gesticulating
    evolving   evoking

    resounding restoring
    recreating renewing

resulting in chemistry's cosmic code
    copying copying copying
resulting in   replication
             mutation
             recombination
resulting in   differentiation
             complexification
             mentation
resulting in   this poem

Tumble

I tumbled off the face of the earth
and fell for years both dark and light
I fell past moments of truth and birth
I felt the rush brush by in flight

the wind robbing me of my breath
the waters roaring at my side
the shadow reminding me of death
the ground recedingly dignified

the sky dims while the stars go bright
the space expands south north west east
the spinning moon passes on my right
stalking the planet that hungry beast

and the other orbs they gather gazing
and watching with curiosity
as I fall past comets' tails all blazing
taking my leave with serenity

the suns bidding me to join their number
to shine with them in desperate burn
and then collapse in cold heavy slumber
all appetite without concern

I pass those fatherless suns and fall
through clouds of particles I cannot name
through memories I cannot recall
through thoughts that I could never tame

I tumbled off the face of the world
a journey without end it seems
life all around me heaved and hurled
spirit singing soft sad joyous dreams

How It Works

the wind gives voice to a thousand tongues
speaking as one
one single word
of mystery
a chorus of green
stretching outwards
singing to the sky
of existence
nothing more than
I am and I am and I am
swaying to the rhythm of creation
standing firm
not through pride or courage
neither stubborn nor defiant
nothing more than a simple integrity
at the base of it all
simply being
I am and I am and I am
and embracing the deep world below
land without light
land of rich decay
grounded in intimate knowledge of death
drawing strength from the darkness
to reach for the light
to be and to be and to be more than I am
expansive
growing
a presence extending
not by anger or appetite
only to be and to be more and more
I am and I am and I am
that is all
I am and I am and I am

Tailors of Eternity

the fashioning of the world
from one moment to the next
in styles both classical and modern
traditional and avant-garde
falls to the hands of the
often overlooked
seldom acknowledged
Tailors of Eternity

making fabric from the firmament
fibers from the mist and fog
white clouds on the whitney gin
storm clouds on the loom
harsh sun rays yielding yarn
soft moonlight making silk
starlight spinning into thread
Tailors of Infinity

sewing zephyrs
weaving will-o-wisps
knitting night and day together
clothing the world in time
they come and they go
following divine patterns

and collecting rags
scraps of cloth
for dressing up souls
in suits of ashes, dust, and clay
and for patching holes
in the human heart

Of Apples and Oranges
Or
A Case of Mistaken Edentity

Said Adam to Eve
Better stop your ribbing
We've got a script to follow
But you keep adlibbing
What do I need with all this resistance?
When what I'm wanting is your assistance

Said Eve to Adam
Don't be such a snake!
A garden needs good care
It's gotta be give and take
What for am I getting all this rejection?
When all I'm needing is a little affection?

Said Adam to Eve
This will bear bitter fruit
Who do you think you're fooling?
In your birthday suit!
Remember, you promised
To love, honor, and obey?
So why do you argue with everything I say?

Said Eve to Adam
I'm not going to bite!
I don't give a fig
If you're looking for a fight
You want I should live in a fool's paradise?
Grow up! Get a job!
Wouldn't that be something nice?

Said God to Adam and Eve
I can't stand the way you bicker!
I made you in my image
Which makes me even sicker
I can't stand to listen to you both
Scream and shout!
I just want some peace and quiet,
So I'm throwing you two out!

Said Adam and Eve to God
Well, that's all right by us!
The service was lousy
We'll be on the next bus!
We need our own place!
There's no privacy here!
We're off now to seek out the primal frontier

Said God to God's self
I think that went well
They'll build their own heaven
They'll dig their own hell
And now I can rest and regain all my glory
'Cause I've some creatin' to do
Over by Alpha Centauri

Aleph

You are the first letter
  of my alphabet

    the lines are neatly drawn
    deep deep within me

      always with me

      already inscribed in me

        before they came to animate
        this envelope of clay

    they were carved beneath the skin
      of my right arm
      and my brow

        written right behind my eyes
        so close I could not see them

    from the beginning
    they brought illumination
      to my inner darkness

        a glowing warmth against the outer chill

        a burning sustained in self-renewal

        a presence felt

        the source beyond my grasp

    your sign engraved upon me

    your stylus cuts me open and I am
      exposed
      revealed

        ashamed of my nakedness

You are the first letter
      of my alphabet

      carved into my heart

      containing memories just out of reach

            one breath
            one single breath

      carried on the wind

            one sweet breath

            and one alone

            and all the rest is commentary

A laugh   like

A leaf

A loft

All left   behind back on the ground

Ah lift   me up if you will

Ah life

Religare

I will bind you up
when you are broken
finding all the shattered pieces
and replacing what is missing
with parts of me

you are my water
I drink deep from your well
you sustain me
envelop me
I ride your waves
in their never ending struggle
with the shore
you fill my lungs
and I return once more

the longing of the soul
is like a prayer
a sacred text
an unseen voice
wanting to draw close
wanting just to touch
holes within the whole
in need of healing
in the fullness of time
we are one

Canaanite Dreams

I am dreaming Canaanite dreams
the rough seas are upon me

I stand transfixed by their primal dance

descending from the mountains
removed from sheltering citadel
I will hide no more in high places

wet sands will be my sanctuary
each day I will build it anew

standing against the shore
trembling before gargantuan force
I bare the markings of the seventh constellation
faint burn from feeble candlelight

coarse freedom my birthright claimed

I take my rest on this day
twelve times twelve generations since
the fires first were kindled

smothered by clouds
the breathless sun
cannot warm the winds
they find me wherever I hide

the waters rise up and
I am touched by
their kiss

Sea Speech

the sea speaks her name
in a roar and a whisper

Do not forget me!

she scratches and bites
carving her name
in rock and sand

Do not forget me!
Do not forget me!

her name is written
in hints of deep longing
in the crash of hard regret
in the pull of distant secrets
in the salt tang of hidden desire

Do not forget me!
Do not forget me!
Return to me once more!

Ellandess

Live
Life
Love
Sing

Life
Long
Song

Love
Life
Sing
Long

Sing
Love's
Song

Life
Left
Sing
Song

Sing
Life's
Song

Love
Left
Song
Lives

Sing
Life
Long

Head First

Head first   she emerges
newly born from the womb of eternity
takes a breath, and trumpets her arrival
crying
        here I am, here I am!

Her name is carved
on the great Tree of Life
whose trunk is a winding
ever-widening scroll
and so begins the cycle of renewal
first days
        a time of awe, and reflection
summer's end, and lessons newly begun

The infant suckles honeyed milk
at her mother's tabernacle breast
she is fed from the first harvest
meals prepared for her in the year now gone
she is schooled in ancient sacred knowledge
beginning in the beginning
with the very first utterance
she learns the secrets of the ox-house line

In winter she comes of age
it is a time of trials
as she takes her place
a daughter
        dutiful and diligent
kindling lights to defend against the darkness
conquering the cold night
with courage and compassion
now sound
and strong
        in mind
        and soul
        and heart

Come spring and she is crowned as Queen
rejoicing as the waters part to let her pass
celebrating freedom and fertility
delighting in life
reveling in sacrament
entering into the covenant of love
sowing seeds for the harvest to come
consecrating herself to the future's conception
she is eager to bear her burden

As summer arrives
weariness sets in
she feels heavy with the passing of days
sadness for all that she has left behind
but
     as well
she feels the warmth of wisdom
and contentment with all
she has achieved
and accomplished

It is time to slow down
     to rest
to prepare for the final labors
so that she may welcome
the daughter
     yet unborn
who will take her autumnal turn
head first   into creation...

Is/Him?

three men appeared along the old stone road
three men appeared   or was it only two?
apparitions standing at my front door
and from their throats I heard a dreadful noise
sweet songs they sang so loud it shook the dust
imaginary silence filled my head
they sat beside the fireplace with me
I don't recall if I let them inside
or if the door had opened on it own
or if they entered by some other means?
we sat around the table and we talked
they spoke in words familiar and yet strange
in unknown harmonies of voices pure
echoes without sound floated in the air
frozen glyphs suspended in fire's glow
I listened as they uttered prophecy
a warning of what soon will come to pass
a vision of disaster to unfold
we shared a meal as we walked down the road
and following the pathway's twists and turns
three travelers and I continued on
by light of brilliant moon   or was it sun?
pavement leading us to the city's edge
two guests departed as we reached the gate
companions gone   I found myself alone
the door was open and I crossed the line
I did not dare to look behind my back
I knew there could be no return for me
I found myself lost in the fog and mist
and what I saw I could not recognize
just colors and patches of dark and light
and emetic odors and scents sublime
I heard the painful beating of my heart
and felt the ground beneath me then give way
I fell   or was I floating up above?
the waters parted   or was it the sky?
to let me pass   I moved at awful speed
so fast I could not catch my breath at all

or was I standing still?   I cannot tell
I saw the end   I saw the tragedy
I shook in fear and terror at the sight
I did not see except in my mind's eye
the threshold crossed   the final agony
revolved like the planets around the sun
a dizzying parabola   and then
I spied their spiral geometric screed
more narrow and more rigid with each pass
or was it deeper and much more profound?
and so time's arrow must come down to rest
to play a lullaby on unstrung bow
and hide beneath the covers of our lies
we dress them up in closure and we smile
and that is all that I can now relate
vapors can be breathed but cannot be grasped
from traces we build buildings to live in
we occupy the skeletons of dreams
and costume them in skins ethereal
believe we are immune to outside harm
ignore the winds we hear beyond the door
and whispers circulating in the room
Two eyes   two ears   but one reality?
deep down we know the world is not like that
catch glimpses now and then of that harsh truth
but well we know that memory's a curse
the blessing of amnesia is our friend
we go about our business to forget
chase pleasure to avoid remembering
make rule to dull our senses and our thoughts
poetry and drama to cloud our minds
myth and faith and science to ease our pain
as we go riding on our beams of light
waving to each other as we pass by
saying   hello   good evening   and good night

Names

My Names

my names precede me
my many names
they were chosen for me
they came before me
not honorifics like nobles of old
although I've earned a few
nor lengthy genealogies
ancestors are   sadly   lost in time
except that I am
the son of the son of the right arm
that they will remember even after I am gone
as I am the father of the same
but there is the name I never had
the second name of the third father
the name that was wrested away
that was conferred upon the people and the land
that was exchanged for roaming mania
byway byline latinated
his trade
his trotter
but if an I offend thee pluck it out
to gain the shortest narrow distance
level plane field
and upper sphere
while first man with feet of clay
is moved to second place
no middle ground for spear pierced focal point
remembering the layer before all else
with divine assistance and initial dropping
a secret identity conferred
reborn in light of tightest focus
but in the voice of the land of angles
true aim and forward fast
true aim and forward fast

Prayer

every breath is a prayer
we pray without knowing
we pray every night and day
Yeah! Hey! Wow! Hey!

giving thanks upon awakening
saying praise in sleep and dreams
breathing in and breathing out
Yeah! Hey! Wow! Hey!

we give thanks for the blessing
we sing praises for the Name
in whispers of the word
Yeah! Hey! Wow! Hey!

we pray all together
we pray when we're alone
in chant and in song
Yeah! Hey! Wow! Hey!

every breath is a prayer
a wind upon the waters
winding through deep passageways
Yeah! Hey! Wow! Hey!

songs of praise and of blessing
borne by the body
carried by the soul
Yeah! Hey! Wow! Hey!

giving thanks for the gift
of life born of love
of love born of life
Yeah! Hey! Wow! Hey!

every breath is a prayer
a sigh of affirmation
springing forth from the source
Yeah! Hey! Wow! Hey!

every breath is a prayer
every pulse is a blessing
every heartbeat a recitation
Yeah! Hey! Wow! Hey!

breathe in and breathe out
every rasp and every gasp
every cry and every whistle
Yeah! Hey! Wow! Hey!

every death is a prayer
one final passage
one last benediction
Yeah! Hey! Wow! Hey!

every breath is a prayer
the spirit's aspiration
rising up to heaven
Yeah! Hey! Wow! Hey!

Yeah! Hey! Wow! Hey!

Yeah!
Hey!
Wow!
Hey!

ONE

Who knows ONE?
Who really knows ONE?
Not one that is one half of two
one third of three
one quarter of four
but ONE and ONE alone
ONE all alone and alone all ONE
ONE that is whole and without limit
a boundless singularity
endless integrity
immeasurable and innumerable
never divided nor duplicated
absolute in unity
complete in infinity
ONE all alone and alone all ONE
ONE that is and will become
the ONE that is to be
dynamic and evolving
alive and ever growing
unique and ever changing
ONE all alone and alone all ONE
Who knows ONE?
Who really knows ONE?
Who can ever ever know ONE?

Just Love, Plain and Simple, and Bittersweet

simple minds
simple measures
simple rhymes
simple pleasures

simple song
simple stories
simple tears
simple worries

simple nights
simple days
simple lives
simple ways

simple thoughts
simple laughter
simple hearts
ever after

Hops-spittle

sleepybed, sleepybed, hops-spittle, home
doctor, no doctor, sad, go home, sad
hurts, go home, hurts, okay! okay!
street! street! sleepybed, home, home, go home
shoes on, I want shoes on
go home, street! street!
all right! all right! hops-spittle, sad
street! street! sad, shoes on
go home, home, shoes on
hops-spittle, hops-spittle, sad, sad, go home
winniethepoohpiglettigger
winniethepoohpiglettigger
home, go home, sleepybed
home, I want home!

Only a Drummer

dancing with my daughter
while Max Weinberg sits in
with the hired band at the fundraiser
playing Springsteen
we could almost pass for normal
for a typical daughter and dad

she loves to dance
we hold hands
and I lead her through some steps I faintly recall
the lindy hop mostly
maybe a touch of hustle and samba
she giggles when I twirl her around
we do some sixties dancing as well
I teach her the hand motions for the Watusi
but she'd rather just hold hands
tightly tightly
holding on

earlier, she had her picture taken
with Governor Corzine
she's such a good poster child
photogenic and easy to pose

before that a couple of my wife's friends
took her with them for a couple of minutes
but she got scared
and they couldn't find my wife
and she started to cry
until they found me
and she held on to me
tightly so very tightly
and I held tight to her
it's our dance of life
from one day to the next
holding on as best we can
holding tightly
and Max Weinberg's only a drummer after all

Slow

for Sarah Strate
on the occasion of her Bat Mitzvah
April 18, 2009

I am not a man of words
no I am not
for I am slow of speech
I am slow
and of a slow tongue
I am slow
I am
slow
the words will not come
the words will not stay
my voice will not carry
I am not a man of words
I am not
not a man
of words
I am slow
slow of speech
and of a slow tongue
tied into knots
I cannot speak well
I am not eloquent
I cannot find the words
I am not understood
I am slow
I am slow
so how can I speak
how can I speak
how can I speak to the god-king?
when I am of a slow tongue
and I am slow of speech
and I am not a man of words
how can I do anything
when I am slow?

your brother will go with you
he will go
go with you
your brother will go with you
to see the god-king
your brother will help you
he will help
will help you
your brother will help you
so you won't be alone
and he will speak your words
yes he will speak
speak your words
the words you cannot
he will be your tongue
when you are slow
he will be your voice
when you are silent
he will speak for you
and you won't be alone
and together you will make miracles
where apart there are none
together in words
and together in acts
together
we will make miracles
when apart there were none

The Ten Commandments

As Told By God to Moses
(A New Translation and Interpretation)

The Buck Stops Here

Use Your Words

But Choose Them With Care

Give Us Both A Break

And Your Parents Too

Respect Life

Family And

Labor As Well

Be Honest And

Be Content

Servitude

we were slaves
we were slaves

building cities for the Pharaoh

if we forget that we were slaves
how can we remember to be free?

Free Pass

at the outer boundary
at the border's edge
who will take the path to freedom?
find the courage to continue?
and who will stay behind
and never know redemption?
and who will arrive too late
swept away by indecision?
and who will begin the journey
but get lost along the way?
and who will lose the will
to continue with the crossing
and turn back again
trying to return
to a home that never was
and no longer can be found?
and who in strength and vigor
and desire and impatience
unable to slow down
not wanting to wait for others
will rush too far ahead
become alone in separation
cut off in isolation
wandering forever
forever wandering?
and who will struggle still
step by halting step
helping one another
carrying those in need
traveling together
climbing hand in hand
passing through trials and hardship
passing through the time of danger
together together as one
to arrive at liberation
to arrive at sanctuary
if only for a while?

Swayed

looking to get a leg up
do you kneel before golden calves?
or is that just some idol talking?
telling you about a tanning game
   of hide and peek?
or do you search for something higher still?

the golden sun in armor blind
in dazzling war on water's run
the horns of cavalry sound defeat
across dried and darkened salt-laced lands
surfaces stretched thin and torn
in service to cosmetic cosmos' holy glow
dry worship of the cleansing sweep

prelude to a protean diet
dissipated deities dressed to kiln
gone through mercurial withdrawal prolonged
playing dust notes scattered in the desiccated air
golden brownian molting love
heir colored to granite grains and bone
fossils cannot form words to speak
cisterns' silence witnessed by primordial blast

yet shelter still exists among soft hills
within damp caverns where once life began
drink deep of cool and shadow and give in
to pale dim domain's comfort and safe home
hidden hope more pleasurable than gold

Inundations

is it conversation or conversion
  that you seeking long for?
dial log in M for the murderous intent
speak your peace be still be calmed
these wars of dark and light
  are yours are yours alone
the battleground within leaves me without
unsettled the encampment
  spawning seeding breeding
enchantment or enchainment
parroting and puppetry
  abound surround confound
your arc's a closing circle
my ark's a refuge floating free
sustaining through catastrophe until
  the armies receding
reveal a sign across the skies the face of God
in every living being
  seen some day may it be some day

Ain' Sof'

the pent-up cost of tongues on fire
five-pointed hallowed caustic calling
what's the prize of all this
fury furor fear or horror
the paranoid strains to make connections
an ecology out of mind
grasping for control in the face of dissolution
orderly imposition by way of inquisition

the answers will not lead you to the
promised land

pyro-piranha consumed with self
as self consumes all else
warship made in own self image
in absence of reflection

the mirror magnifies
turns light to heat
the heat rises
but does not lead to heaven
your melting gods do not reside above
where lava flows there is no life

it is a well known fact
that the flash of justice is blinding to the eye
that the sudden blast of peace is deafening
that the rough honey of compassion stills the
    hurried tongue
that the cool jazz of communion will heal all
    blistered thought

the quest for understanding is
a journey of a lifetime
do not mistake your
resting place for final resolution

infinity is not a number

Solar Eclipse

The eyeless gaze sees
    false lies surface slow
    lines curve and crook upon
    tongues sweet stinging stick
    hands a mesmer misdirect
    feet a maze a motion fast
    a feline feral dance
    a dizzying catastrophe
    drunken deep delights a daze
    being beautiful as nightfall
    cast straight shine cuts baldly blind
    captivated capitated carried away

The eyeless gaze sees through
    the laughter
    the mock
    crowding cruel
    crows and fingers
    pointing poking prodding piercing
    How they revile you when you're weak
    How they despise you when you're strong

The eyeless gaze sees true
    to memory and justice
    Listen   Listen
    a voice to guide you through the dark
    O Judge   have courage and conviction
    O Guardian   keep faith in lonely sacrifice
    O Champion   bring down pillars of deceit
    O Child   come now walk with me

Is Saul Among the Prophets?

Is Saul among the prophets?
those whom the divine would wish destruction?
he dances a prayer and chants an apparition
he is unstuck from calendar and chronicle
breathing vapors of a strange strange fire
building bricks of mud and straw
towering warrior   brooding over Ur-text
speaking ancient tongues of Babel
floating freely upon flood waters
knocking on the gates of Eden
naked and unashamed   demanding admission
no answer   no acknowledgement
from silent angels standing guard
gates shut tight against him
he cries out
despair and desperation
weeping witches feed him
mushroom stew and nocturnal shade
he is scalded by the priestly presence
he sees his house collapsed and turned to ash
he hears heavenly voices
could they be nothing more
than echoes of his own rage driving him
to drive away the ones he loves the most?
no mercy   no forgiveness   no justice
only sword and spear
and so many wounds   so deep   so deep within
abandoned and defeated   longing for an end
he does not know if he was meant to be the lion
or the sacrificial lamb
all he knows is lamentation
O how the mighty have fallen
O how the mighty have fallen
O how the mighty have fallen
and yet he finds that he is now
among the prophets
among the prophets
among the prophets   freed from pain

My Ancestor

my ancestor
some sixty generations ago
slew a giant in his youth
sang songs of love and devotion
was bathed in a rare ointment
became a mighty warrior
led soldiers to victory
slaying tens of thousands
united tribes into a great kingdom
conquered a citadel on a mountain
made it his shining city
was loved by his people
was loved by his God
was loved by his women
had many wives
abused his power and position
was betrayed by a son that he loved dearly
survived and reigned for forty years
was filled with lust for all his days and nights
had many, many children
many more grandchildren
many many more great grandchildren
many many many more descendants
millions alive today
many wearing his shield
my ancestor
had beautiful eyes

Gulf

So spoke Qohelet:

sing to me beloved
  of the loneliness of Eden
the garden standing empty
  gently longing for the day
of healing and return

weeping waters whisper
  of embraces that are broken
of the missing touch
  of a responsive hand
four thin extended fingers
  framing sacred vision
of exile's final ending
  of a new noesis
of an eon of one

Open the gates
                  Open the gates
                                    Open the gates
Sweeter than honey
                              Sweeter than wine
          The day to come
          The day to come

Ghetto

And we rock and sand go into the furnace
forming reddened skin flexing flowing free
adapting to the shape
the shape of necessity
tempered
tempered and purified
in this oven   in these flames
until the fires are bartered for the light
silver streams now fixed and frozen
frozen mirrored to reflect/deflect
clear fluid now made cool and hard
hard windowed to look out/look in
as judgment arrives in the wake of heat:
And who shall be a dagger?
And who shall be a shield?
And who a looking glass?
And who will magnify the small?
And who will see beyond the stars?
And who will carry it all within
to contain to protect to preserve?

Five Windows

I am not of the community   no
not a remnant half-remembered
in museumed persistence   no
but I will tell their story just the same
it's a story that you'll want to hear
that every cold-cultured conqueror
could stand to learn

do not close your gates
like the covers of a book
the future remains free of any rule

On a Walking Tour

And so we return
to the places of our pain
to see the gates that once imprisoned us
to marvel at our misery

But the blood has turned to dust
and blown away
the air has been cleared of confinement's stench
and we have long been cleansed
of accusations of guilt
and designations of shame
looking on now out of curiosity alone
thinking on how far we all have come
forgetting how it is we still remain
prisoners of the age to which we all are born

Fortune

all alone and alarmed
left behind
lost
and fallen into
strange terrain I
followed an uncertain
alleyway and there I
found a sign
words trans-
forming foreign to
familiar
finding footsteps from those who
came before
fathers and mothers
pointing the way
forward to return
guiding me to where
they could not go
leading me to escape the land
to climb high to
freedom

Assembly of the Faithful (Jubilee x3)

written for the sesquicentennial celebration
of Congregation Adas Emuno of New Jersey

Jubilee   Jubilee   Jubilee
come join our sacred community
we journeyed across the land and sea
to a place where we could all breathe free

    assembly of the faithful
    gathering in celebration
    we are joyful   we are grateful
    for our home and congregation

Jubilee   Jubilee   Jubilee
we honor our living legacy
keep alive our ancient memory
and renew our shared identity

    assembly of the faithful
    built on a strong foundation
    of learning   prayer   and justice
    we affirm our dedication

Jubilee   Jubilee   Jubilee
may God grant us peace and harmony
and sustain us through each century
and bless and keep us all lovingly

    assembly of the faithful
    in glad commemoration
    praising those who came before us
    hear now our proclamation

Jubilee   Jubilee   Jubilee
we join in devotion loyally
in defense of human dignity
and all of Creation's majesty

assembly of the faithful
hear now our confirmation
to remain steadfast and true
from generation to generation

Jubilee   Jubilee   Jubilee
planting seeds for harvests yet to be
building on our storied history
together assembling faithfully

Kol Nidre

Forgive me
my foolishness
my failures
my false assurances

the weeping cello's melody

Forgive me
my fabrications
my forgeries
my facsimiles

called forth from the depths of penitent hearts

Forgive me
my fickle wants
my futile reach
my fevers and favors

rises to the gates of divine redemption

Eight Lights

One
Light
For
Liberty
Freedom from slavery and tyranny
From oppression and persecution
Freedom to live in harmony
With the Earth and with Heaven

One
Light
For
Law
Justice and equality
Human rights and human dignity
Peaceful coexistence
An end to war and violence

One
Light
For
Leaders
To stand up for liberty and bow to the law
To lead by example with courage and wisdom
To be a hammer that builds
As well as a hammer of war
With a passion for peace
For justice
and
For freedom

One
Light
For
Letters
Four on a dreidel
Twenty-two in total
Infinite in combination
Endless in education
An alphabet aligned with order
A numbering of our works, days, names
Books—greater than any leader
Knowledge stored transcends our times

One
Light
For
Learning
Reading, writing, remembering
Studying, questioning, understanding
Preserving tradition
Saving continuity from being lost
Moving forward—evolution
Avoiding errors of the past
Teachers—the highest calling
Bring to the world much needed healing

One
Light
For
Life
A sacred gift
Most precious of all
Vessel of the spirit
Root of liberty and law

One
Light
For
Love
Courtship and Family
Friends and Neighbors
Community and Humanity
Creation and Creator

One
Light
For
Laughter
Spinning dreidels
Chocolate gelt
Jelly doughnuts
Potato latkes
Giving gifts
Singing songs
Saying blessings
Children playing
Family visiting
Friends gathering
Lifting hearts
Kissing keppellahs
Glowing candles
Eight nights
Eight lights
Happy Chanukah!

Conversation

we're all relative	Albert Einstein said
it's all in your head	Sigmund Freud replied
we're only human	Hannah Arendt declared
you and I are it	Martin Buber observed
there's no escape	Harry Houdini insisted
it's only natural	Baruch Spinoza explained
it's the system	Franz Kafka cried
class is in session	Karl Marx announced
just play fair	Leon Trotsky answered
and work hard	Samuel Gompers affirmed
change it up	Emma Goldman proclaimed
write it down	Gertrude Stein emphasized
I must be going	Groucho Marx asserted
watch your back	Anne Frank warned
don't forget	Marcel Proust reminded
keep the beat	George Gershwin maintained
don't act out	Sarah Bernhardt advised
show me how	Louis B. Meyer contended
it's all a game	John von Neumann responded
make it fast	Sandy Koufax demanded
don't think twice	Bob Dylan directed
stand tall	Betty Friedan averred
stick together	Emile Durkheim exclaimed
heal the world	Jonas Salk pleaded
try to be free	Leonard Cohen counseled
love's the answer	Emma Lazarus concluded

Callings

Poetry/Perception/Prayer

Standing
Naked
Open
Vulnerable

Facing
The Full Force
Of The Total Environment

Answering
Here I Am
I Am Ready

When You Call My Name

will it be sudden?
will it be slow?
will I see it coming?
or just not know?
will there be pain?
will there be bliss?
or just a fall
into nothingness?
will there be darkness?
will there be light?
will I come quietly?
or put up a fight?
when you call my name
will I heed your voice?
like a well-trained dog?
will I have no choice?
or will I resist
like a willful child
who has grown overtired
and become wild?
will I be angry
when you call
and curse your name
or try to stall?
will I say too soon!
and resent it?
will I say I've sinned!
and repent it?
when you call my name
will I be filled with fear
and tremble and shake
as you draw near?
or will I be warmed
by the glow of your face
and filled with love
in your embrace?

Sustain

do not wash this stain from me
let it sink into my skin
let it mark me for all time
I won't deny it
won't disguise it
let it reach the heart of me

do not wash this stain from me
let it sink into my skin
I embrace it
smell it, taste it

no shame, no sorrow
no regrets
no lusting for forgiveness

no

do not launder or purify me
do not render or sterilize me
keep me from the water and flame
and let the soil surround my soul

do not wash this stain from me
let it sink into my skin
let it mark me for all time
becoming now a part of me
a sign burned through the heart of me
in being be all that is me

Breath

the angel of death
and the avatar of life
battled for his breath

this might be the end
the doctor says to his wife
it's a downward trend

medical machines
monitored his slow decline
displayed on their screens

tears well in her eyes
she sobs and begs for a sign
of hope in disguise

she prays to her God
not yet not yet please more time
sees the doctor nod

we've done all we could
there is no reason or rhyme
things just don't look good

struggling to inhale
each breath being a lifetime
heart about to fail

life's avatar said
his passing would be a crime
what a life he led

death's angel replied
mercy is my mission here
grace for those who've died

between life and death
there is courage and there's fear
poised between each breath

l Sack/Cloth and Ashes

the binding of the future
tied at the wrists and ankles
laid out upon the altar
the altared future bound
and readied for the sacrifice
to sacrifice the future
on the altar that is present
bound upon the altar
so to cut the future's throat
the draining of the future
blood spilled upon the altar
and the kindling has been gathered
and the wood is set on fire
the burning of the future
for to make a sacrifice
scapegoat upon the altar
the future a burnt offering
the flames reach high above us
the smoke lifts up to heaven
to appease the lofty powers
to be pleasing to the eyes
the binding of the future
the burning of tomorrow
on the altar of today

Essenic Route?

abstinence makes
the heart grow fonder
the mind stronger
the soul larger still

discipline
control
mastery of the self
gained by power of the will

Soap

sacrificed on your altar
to satisfy your need for cleansing
I give of myself to you
and slowly I disappear and die for you

I Fell

leash tangled
cutting into ankles
knees smashed into concrete
knuckles ripped in self-defense
shoulder hurts bad
but why?

Reversals of Fortune

Fire
Ice
Bang
Whimper
Beast

this life
this world
this time
must pass away
and darkness
will demand
to have its day
what has commenced
must surely
surely cease
the tightest grip
must also know
release
but still we must
as much as we may
reverse evil–live
or so I pray

Prayer for Thanksgiving

this time of year is set apart
as a time of Thanksgiving in our land
and we certainly ought to give thanks
for living in a land of great abundance
but we can only give thanks
when we give thanks to someone
when we give thanks to a higher power
so we give thanks to You, God
we give thanks to You

and it is easy enough to give thanks to You
for those of us who live comfortable lives
who have our health, and the love of family and friends
who have clothing to wear and a roof over our heads
and more than enough to eat
not to mention some measure of material wealth

and for those of us whose lives are not blest by such abundance
or whose lives are touched by sickness, tragedy, or isolation
it still may be easy to give thanks
if we have found spiritual fulfillment
inner peace and outer contentment

for all of us who feel some form of satisfaction with our lives
it is a time when we ought to be recalling our good fortune
and recounting our blessings
and giving thanks for all that we have received
it takes so little effort
for us to do it for ourselves
we need no one else to speak on our behalf

and that is why, God
that I do not want to speak now
for the self-satisfied and the satiated
and instead I want to give voice
to those among us who are angry at You
yes, angry at You, God
and for that reason find it hard to give thanks
at this time of year
or any other

I want to give voice for those among us who are angry at You
because some of us seem to get more than our fair share
of sadness and affliction
more than our share
of pain, hardship, and tragedy
because the burden You have placed on some of us
seems so much heavier
than what You have asked the rest of us to carry
because the world that You created
sometimes seems so unjust, arbitrary, even cruel

and I want to speak for those of us who are angry at You, God
because we see evil triumphant
oppression and murder rule the day
because hate, aggression, and violence go unanswered
because there seems to be no punishment for the wicked
no reward for those who do justly, love mercy, and walk
   with humility
because the innocent go to unmarked graves without number
and because even at the best of times, Your angel of death
   haunts our days

and I want to talk to You, God
on behalf of those of us who are angry with You
because our prayers seem to go unanswered
because Your silence is overwhelming
because Your eclipse leaves us in the dark
because Your absence leaves a void in the human soul
that no science, philosophy, or politics can hope to fill

I want to say a prayer, God, on behalf of those among us
   who are angry at You
and find it difficult to give thanks
wanting instead only to ask You

why?

in our tradition
it is no sin to question God
to debate God
to argue with God
so why should it be a sin to be angry at God?

and just as there are times
when we ask God to put aside anger
and grant us forgiveness
there are times when we too need to put aside our own anger
and forgive God
to forgive You, God, for not living up to our
   expectations and fantasies
to forgive You, God
for not being the God that we want You to be
for instead being the God that You are
to forgive You, God
for not being an overprotective parent
and instead being a partner
and leaving it up to us to finish what You started
to complete Your creation
to repair reality
to heal the world
and if we find it in our hearts to forgive You, God

then maybe
maybe then
we can all of us find it in our hearts to give thanks
for what we have received

for the gift of life
  however brief and troublesome
  still, life itself is a miracle

for our bodies
  through which we can enjoy
  pleasure and delight

for our senses
  through which we can encounter
  great beauty, and wonder

for our feelings
  through which we can know
  love, and joy, and hope

for our minds
  through which we can learn and grow
  acquire knowledge
  gain understanding
  seek wisdom
  and find meaning

for our spirit
  through which we can experience
  the sacred and the sublime
  the holy and the holistic
  transcendence and communion

for the universe
  through which we can experience
  connection across time and space

for others like ourselves
  from whom we can draw comfort and strength
  with whom we can form communities
  gaining commitment and purpose

for the chance to make things better than
  they were before
to contribute
  even in the smallest of ways
to be a part of something greater
  so much greater
  than ourselves

and so, it is for these gifts above all else
which You have provided to all of us
to each and every human being
we give thanks to You, God
we give thanks to You

Ignite

spark
  floating in the dark
drifting down to ground
  ember
glowing faint but true
  cradled by currents
nourishing breath
  soft winds sing a lullaby
of a time to come
  when a flame will rise
ember does not understand the words
  but takes comfort from the melody
as the song says someday
  ember will ignite and send
sparks
  floating in the dark
drifting down to ground
  to become embers
glowing faint but true
  someday to bring about
an end to night

Fear

living in fear
you will never be free
and the prison you dwell in
will be the one you create
no dungeon is deeper
than the depths of a soul
that lives without courage
in dread of the dark
and alarmed by the light

some spirits are broken
by all that they've seen
all that they've gone through
all that they've done
they deserve our compassion
they deserve our care
but we can't let them guide us
their vision is blurred

those ruled by worry
those ruled by dread
those ruled by horror
and those ruled by despair
are ruled by tyrants
and never content

the demand for safety
is an unquenchable thirst
no matter how much
you manage to drink
you will always want more
do not drown in those waters

there cannot be life
unless there is risk
there cannot be growth
unless there is death
we can't be afraid
for there to be trust
we have to be daring
if we want to know love
we must defy terror
if we want to know peace

and no it's not easy
no one said it would be
to see in each other
sparks of energy divine
glowing with light
within earthly vessels
fractured and flawed

but the answer is simple
one we've known all along
do not do what is hateful
be merciful and just
be humble and brave
do not live in fear
for what might be
but live in respect
for all that there is
and live in hope
for what yet may be

My Ana Marred

for Aung San Suu Kyi

your mightiest ships
cannot sail to heaven on
a river of blood

Idylls of Mars

idly by   idly by
lazy river red
let it pass
pouring along
soil fertile drunk
on dark waters

brother   can you see?
lay it down now
float along

sister   can you hear?
soft breezes
passing into silence

close your eyes now
and hum a mingled melody
calm recollections
memories to please
singing
all well
all well now
all well in the end

standing   standing
so quiet and still
idly by   idly by
idly by

Memorial Day 2009

i.

it all seems so simple
it all seems so clear

bury the dead, and tend to the wounded
cry for the innocent
mourn   and grieve   and comfort
remember the fallen
and their comrades
survivors
record their names
recall their lives
celebrate their service
recognize their courage
and say
no more
and let all of us say
no more
and let every man and woman and child say
no more
and let all the world join together as one and say
no more

ii.

the dark gods demand that we practice ritual human sacrifice like
the idol worshippers of old so that we might purify ourselves by
the shedding of blood

to purify by blood by blood by blood of the innocent and blood
of the guilty blood of kin and blood of strangers blood of enemies
and blood of friends blood of the hated and blood of the loved
blood of neighbors both near and far

all must be sacrificed for the thirst of the dark gods is without
limit and the hunger of the dark gods never ceases so the bodies
are burnt upon the altar called destruction as offerings for the
feast of the dark gods

in the name of the dark god Mar in the name of the dark god
Tyr in the name of the dark god Are in the name of the dark
god War we sacrifice sons and daughters brothers and sisters
husbands and wives fathers and mothers to you

iii.

this is not a perfect world
this is not a perfect world
this world will never be perfect

Eros may never erase Eris
there will always be strife and discord
but do we have to let them rule over us?

this is not a perfect world
this is not a perfect world
this world will never be perfect

but we can make things better

we can build bridges
we can build buildings
we can build bombs
so why can't we build justice and compassion?
why can't we build peace and sanity?
why can't we build a new way forward for humanity?

it all seems so simple
it all seems so clear

No Man's Land

an island called His
an island called Hate
an island called Hope?

Heat Waves Goodbye

sweet Joan of Arc cried out:
my God! if they'd burn me
they'd burn anybody

> the inferno has no off switch
> Oswiecim is a machine
> that runs on its own

Maria Curie looked up from her pierogies
and nodded in agreement
holding up her hands to show off her
  blackened tan

> between life and afterlife
> there is a purgatory called half-life
> where heretical visions obscure the
>   cataracts buried underground

Brigitte Bardot would melt your eyes out
she looked so heavenly in her Bikini
but will they call her a saint
  five centuries from now?

Still

Residue of a dream
      walking words of prayer
            sung in soft shadow speech
                  celebrating love and life
                        revealing lore   law   and learning
                            divining celestial signs and ciphers

Residue of a dream
             enchanted chain of blessings
                 living links to time's awakening
                     forged by faith   holding fast

Residue of a dream
             wandering among you
                 unnoticed   unremarked

but still here

Wilderness

Sand

the obsessions of others oppress me
their compulsions repulse me
valorous recession beckons
but I stand frozen
listening to listings
disassociated spinnings
dizzying crossings
items, lines, and me

send the anesthesia of amnesia
and not this recklessly thin nostalgia
sweet odor of rot
cheerful decomposition
whistling sound of the empty spaces within
these maggots seek to hollow me out
O how they love me so
gluttons feeding on my guts

when comes an expiration to these aspirations?
all I ask is that you bury me deep
in the cleansing sands
of my ancestors
let dear desiccation whither me down
shrunken and shedding the stench of their hands

when will you call an end to all this schismogenesis?
splinters of the brilliant and the blind
fractures of expectancies and remembrances
gashes of secessions and seditions
wounds of separations and severities
all all can be sealed repaired healed

the digit of God is an integer
touching us to form a ratio
to everything we shall assign a reason
and a rhyme to every purpose under heaven

there is no joy without a joining
no joining unless adjoining
we collect ourselves and forge swords of identity
one tribe
one totem
one taboo
to do no harm
and all the rest is commentary
an uphill elevation
struggling to ascend
an uprising to find our freedom
to find a loving home
not within fixed walls
but in the folds of our tents
and the flows of our rounds
cycles of departure and return
ceaseless turnings
ebbings and floods alike bringing
erasure

I stand before a jury of my fears
overcome by guilt
my inner sense denied
before I return to the cry I am seen
heavy dense weighs upon me
ponderously preposterously preposthumously
humanely I request solitary confinement

I am no Christian soldier
to turn the other cheek
and then return with an army at my back
I have only my wits and words
my pen and papers
my needle and thread
embroidered embroiled
embossed embassied

I did not write these laws
I can only tell you what they do not say
I interpret the intervals between
your rules and your rulers
your margin of aura
to air is human
is it not?

I cannot measure the deep rave you are engaged in
but I witness it all
one eye to see across all time and space
the other to magnify the minutia of existence
but where where is the perspective?

I listen to your mad dreams of milk and grain
and decipher the warnings of your own unconsciousness
projecting your desires and rages
onto a screen made of skin
a tattoo of light reading
items, lines, and me

forsake eye and ego
to speak the truth now
declare the verdict
speak verities and verifications
versions and variations
visions and viewpoints
virtualities rally true
you to me

I face my accusers
without excuses
no recusing the elusively reckless recluse
you're on her
all risible
rising above it all
I can't stand the condemnation
when you haven't even read me my writes

you pass judgment
like passing the bottle
and I feel the burn
the buzzing blinding effinall
drunken power
Dr. Jerk'll tan your hide at the saloon Mister
so say good night Mary
and wake me if I scream
or if you've heard this one before
I walk into a bar and the bartender says
we don't get many of your kind in here
so I leave as I arrived
disbarred
no baritone and losing my tenor all too easily
as soap ran noses off
better wipe 'em clean
erasure

if you meet the baby Buddha at a fork in the road
cut him in two
or so says wise kinky solo man
with all that jazz a bell ringing in his ears
who was it that split the Adam?
parted the Red Sieve?
shaped clay into men and mountains?
cooled fires into women and waters?
poured love and loneliness into the world
polarities giving rise to circuitous motion
fluid dynamics
sacred ecologies
first and second natures?

nurturing laws of divine compassion
not regal legations of profane confusion
I have no wish to be of the Roman Empire
I wear no boots made to conquer and crush
my feet are bare and sore from walking
wandering the deserted streets of my city

I will fight
I will defend
and I will fail
and fall to your hectoring taunts and trials
you can drag my body all around
you know no boundaries
berserk amok lost to red
your inferno consumes from within
is there nothing human left?
not even greed envy hate?
just an engine commanding slaves to shovel
and be shoveled
into its furnace
into ashes within ashes
into dust within dust real revolutions
overturn internment
into stovepipe smokestack
nothing says loving like something in the oven commandant
bellies swelled with pride
from consuming child

again reveal cowering secrets
tell all then toss them aside
the vast silences of the barren and the sterile
do not rip these words from me
some things are best unsaid
stillborn

I am no wolf's cub
no adopted son
my tribe is small
but our music pleases celestial ears
I sing
of the frenzies of power
of the wounds of wealth
of the ruins of piety
and of mercies that yet may come

I was not born to the birthright
but earned it by strength of mind
by learning
by planning
by the beauty of sacrifice
by the courage of love
by will
by ability
to question
debate and disagree
by skepticism and negation
I prove humanity
deny brutality
end slavery

to be forced to serve cruel masters
is not easily forgotten
you are wise to dread
the ones you seek to intimidate dominate
for you who own slaves
shall become as slaves yourselves
the slaves of slaves
claimed by the ones you claim to own
set to serving your servants
prisoners of those you have imprisoned
captivated by the ones you hold captive

and so we came to that mountain of wondrous
   signs and horrible portents
and you illuminated all that may come to pass
written in letters of cold blue flame
carved upon my temple
words of truth and life
animating this poor lump of clay
you breathe your name into us all
and we are one
though we have forgotten
the sound of you

and what dark force led us
to become as cattle
fattened for the sacrifice
led to the slaughter
grazing upon the grasses of the field
suckling upon the teats of beasts
cowed and crowded into the cities of our masters?

go shun these army ghettoes
and shed the pale skin of these militant settlements
there is no oasis in this cold cold desert

have you forgotten that the seasons have no regard
for the sovereignty of the sun
and instead attend upon
the grace and glory of the moon?
have you forgotten that the day begins
with evening's song
and ends with shadow's conquest of the hills?

there is no return from history
having forsaken garden and guardian for two-car garage
and gadgetry in endless abundance

eating from the tree of knowledge
they were struck dumb
eating from the tree of life
they were struck dead
but continued on unknowing
unmindful of their final status
expecting fruition from their best laid
gangland plans
graveyard plots
goal line stands
frozen custard and ices outside of the umber toned
   clam house
mum's the word and lips sealed forever
and the lie lacks credibility
we will all sing a gallow's song
Joey, Bobby, and me

organization is protection
we build walls and armies
only to find that we have
conquered and captured ourselves
our world it seems is hollow
and one day it will implode
so much anger anger all around
demanding energy motion action
a universe expanding
a conquering empire
an unstoppable engine
an intractable epidemic
engulfing the earth
Nemesis feeding the Furies on the Grapes of Wrath
and what remedy can you prescribe program?
repress suppress and it returns tenfold

the only salvation is in the sands
their summons to seek shelter
in their fire flow
follow the unmarked trail
the footsteps erased
the signs unseen
just listen listen close
only sounds can save you now
only music can lead you
through the indifferent terrain

where can we find guides
who act for the group and not for gain?
can we learn the lesson of the sand
to be a particle within a wave
exist in relativity
neither absolute nor unanchored
but in relation operation instruction?

categories are not logic
clarity is not vision
calculation is not decision
drifting falling scattered
in sacred suspension
weightless against the coming storm
dreaming ever dreaming
who sends these dreams unbidden?
who sends these night Maries to my bed?
I do not miss my nocturnal omissions
my deceased is in remission
and walks again
and speaks to me now
without a voice
I strain to hear your silences

did you think that my path here
was strewn with rose petals and cherry blossoms?
the red you see is the color of life's blood upon
    the broken glass
and the rust of old machinery
all ground down down down
into the softness of sands

the old neighborhood
is not what it once was
after uncounted crucifixions
cruelty written upon the skins of my ancestors
items, lines, and me

whipped into a frothy frenzy
upon abominable abdomens
abducted domains
damn yell in the rebellion's den
a cry of warning born in mourning
all that noise cannot drown out
the sound of your idle whispers
the counting of the omerta
in ciphers and codes
you try to go from alpha to omega
with your Roman numerals

and cannot understand why
the percentages come out wrong
but there is nothing you cannot measure
with the point of your sword
the accordion note is cut
right in front of your eyes
as one goes into one yielding none
and from there you can derive
your algebraic jihad

sandstorm scours the lands
a blast that cleanses and cremates
sand and ash become blackened glass
another obsidian city where
the streets flow red from young sacrifice
no peace or comfort there
they do not speak the language of dreams
despise the deep meanings that elude
the crushing certainties of their logic
shattered mirrors reflecting bits and pieces of surfaces
fatal accidents occidents incidents decedents
their soldiers are teeth aligned
ready to bite rip chew
in their sanguine hunger
theirs is a song for sour eyes and tindered ears
toys for the monster child that hides within
born of fever
cold sweat on acid skins
the night marred by evil visions
the baker sent to the gallows
the bearer of cups set free
the dreamer imprisoned
and in command
christening of the fist
in armor giddy
gathering at the mountain
surrounded by the hills
the war to end the war to end all wars
has never ended

ruled by your slave selves
led by your imprisoned egos
how can I serve such incapacity?
capaciously decapitated
an acephalous society
will never get ahead
you say hurry now chop chop
but my path is blocked at every turn
the signs reduced to scribblings
uncounted unnumbered unencumbered
items, lines, and me

I am but a groveling footnote
yearning to be set free
but I fear we find ourselves
at cross references
our language is confounded
our citizens confused
our children scattered
they wander the sands
there is no safety in citadels
no protection in bunkers
flame rains down on us from the skies
the mountains collapse upon us
the earth seizes up and swallows us
the waters gather together to take us
and what manager minister administrator shall we turn to
for salvation solutions solace?
what policies procedures shall be put in place
to address the situation?
how will memos forms spreadsheets be heard on high?

your towers of transmission
dishes of reception
satellites overhead
banks of data down below
are you so very proud of them?

will your desert of bits and bytes save you from the
    sands of time?
or do you place your faith in the binding and melting
    of grains and gravels
into cement, glass, and asphalt?

enslaved to make monuments
your thoroughfare rows and columns
your grid and lock will not contain them
these particles will slip through
cast your nets to work they will not
arising all will turn back to sand and depart
and the messengers will descend upon you
with hunger and thirst
swarming locusts
and how will you exit this night mire?
having sold your soul to the wind O so breezily
will you now repeat or repent
your own O so twisted whirlwind?

my limbs hang limp
my lungs rip and rend
my heart cracks
and I am betrayed by brutal études
they have their marching orders
turning tides to suit their whims
without memory there is no integrity
and so I become an unmade man
hit me up sin eaters
and end this tiring rant
a fever is no revelation
a reverie is not a vision from beyond
the random firings of neurons is not the divine will made manifest
and poetry poetry is not prophecy
I cannot exceed the parameters of my programming
I am infinite yes but bounded
inhumane bondage
a closed system looping back upon itself
again and again and again

spill it out
compile it
seal it up between the covers of a book
items, lines, and me

redeem me as you would a coupon
put a price on my head
discount me if you must
I am currency
exchange me
I am spent
consumed from within
I am a bubble
watch me pop
there I go

write just rage
it's a cage to dwell in
trapped in endless recursions
cursing the dark course
that they laid out for themselves
do not blame me then for my departure
I have paid my toll
now let me pass
I have done as much as I could
with the materials available to me
and the circumstances surrounding me
I will not apologize for my limitations imperfections impermanencies
all that I could create was a moment in time
that could only pass away
the mightiest monuments and the greatest edifices
fold up like tents as we move on
and all that remains all that remains all that remains
is the sands
flowing flowing going back and forth
forming and deforming
dunes and depressions
at the whim of the winds
but never at their mercy

they care nothing for your economies and finance
for your hierarchies and bureaucracies
for your borders and papers
for your positions and titles
does each and every grain of sand have a sign
designating its individuality?
if so
then who could know them all?
who could call each one by name?
who can know the multitudes
count the innumerable
take the measure of the infinite?
is there one
in divided dualities
who can be an integrity?

we learn to speak so we can demand
        look at me
and forever after we are motivated by such longings
        listen to me
so we begin life
and spend our days
calling out in this fashion
seeking divine audience
or the next best thing
it is not thought that confirms existence
that's putting Descartes
in front of
the horse's mouth
a kick in the head
it is being seen and being heard
that is believing
it is in your eyes that I see myself
it is in your answer that I hear my words
water quenches more than thirst
as the shallow flower child learns
to his regret:

still water brings reflection
　　　　the trap of self
　　　　the alienation of knowing
　　　　the end of action

flowing water brings voice
　　　　the joy of song
　　　　the embrace of speech
　　　　the current of memory

frozen water brings peace
　　　　the quiet of rest
　　　　the numbness of sleep
　　　　the expansion of dreams

and the rain
　　　　the rain
　　　　the rain
　　　　the rain brings love
　　　　the comfort of touch
　　　　the rhythm of attention
　　　　the strength of awakening

I am awash with blessings
soaked to the bone
immersed in your providence
my cups run me over
bathed in the sound of your glory
I fear that I shall be drowned out

I did not ask for favor
I did not ask to be chosen
I did not seek out this burden
but how could I say no?
how how how could I refuse?
I must find the desert in this ceaseless oasis
the quiet amidst these discordant pastures
the spaces between the writings between the pages between the
items, lines, and me

escape the depths upon me
crushing crushing me
find the protean sands
the messengers of time
how they try to bottle you up
place scorpions in a jar
to watch them strike
their strife is poison
toxic plumes decorate
birds of a featherweight
lacking substance but not harm
they stake their heartfelt claims
seeking succor
they cry cry cry for their wounded pried wide open selves
esteeming hot
needy dough
rising expanding appearances suggesting a grand fabrication
but full of holes
mostly air on the inside
I have no time for such extensions aggrandizements
empires are flimsy things that so easily implode
my time grows short
I must move on
I cannot wait
and so will content myself
with flatbread
anyway it's easier to pack
and I have a long journey ahead of me

I grow weak from poison
the bitter taste in my mouth
will not depart from me
until I myself find escape
from these constructions
that burn and collapse
find a way around
these obstructions
find a way through this
careless destruction
get out before
the last engulfing eruption

there is no rapture in ruptures
divide the waters
divide the lands
as you see fit but
no conquest will last
no empire will endure
no citadel will remain unconquered
no tower will stand forever
know now what was never understood
by Ozzie or Oswald or any of us
know now what mandates us
that fame flies off
that power consumes itself
that wealth wastes away
that only the sands remain
particles forming waves
ever ever eternal in motion
let us flow as they do
around curved spaces
wandering all around
not in straight lines but loops
going forth
only to return again
the circular motion is everlasting
direction without aim
restless as the ocean
still as the mountains
in patterns that persist
from the subatomic to the stars
this, this, this, this, this
this, this, this, this
this, this, this
this, this
this
is what we are

Words

Born Within a Shadow

my parents survived the Holocaust
that pretty much puts everything else into perspective
no matter how bad things get for me
how can I complain?
and it's a hard thing to live up to
that your life is somehow supposed to redeem
all that was lost
a messiah in miniature
and it's hard to live with the guilt
of not having survived some great ordeal
my parents wouldn't say much about it
wouldn't go into details
how do you speak to your children about such things?
but it was always with us
an unspoken, unseen presence
felt in the nerves, always nerves
in worry, fear, and anger
and in the nerves, the nerves, the nerves
in a nervous, cautious, overprotective kind of nurture
knowing how flimsy and fragile the world is
how quickly things can change
how vulnerable we all are
how precious life can be
I learned to be the calm one
my parents met after the war, as refugees
if they had never been displaced
I never would have been born
how strange it is to know
that I owe my life to calamity and catastrophe
how strange it is to be born from flames
that never burned me
to be born out of ashes
that never touched me
to be born within a shadow
whose source I could never see

Almost Australian

nationality is a funny thing
my father was Hungarian, born before the First World War
in a place called Transylvania which
after the war, became a part of Romania
my mother's family came from Russia, or rather, from Ukraine
running away from the Communists
she was born on the border between Moldavia and Bessarabia
officially listed as Romanian
but she grew up in Poland
my parents met and were married in Paris
in the wake of the Second World War
they were refugees, stateless
when I was little, I used to stare at a fold-up set of
    attached postcards
crisp, black and white images of the City of Lights
the Arc de Triomphe in particular caught my eye
there was something about its geometry
and its ornate exterior
that I found captivating
my parents could not get into the United States
where my mother had family
because of immigrant quotas
so they went to Australia instead
and lived in Sydney for three years
before the quotas changed
and they came to New York
my father was fifty
my mother was forty
I guess at that point it was now or never
so I was born soon after that
and instead of a teddy bear
I had a koala bear
and there were little souvenirs around the house
a small boomerang
a kangaroo pen and ashtray set
and I was told that I could have been born in Australia
which I accepted
as all children assume
the inevitability rather than the improbability
of their own birth

Thank You for the Books

I was born on the Island of Manhattan
two weeks later we moved to the Island of Long
to the Greater New York City Borough of Queens
to a neighborhood known as Kew Gardens
to an apartment on the sixth floor
in a building on the corner of 82nd Avenue
and Queens Boulevard
across from Borough Hall
and the courthouse and the prison
and above the subway
where the E and the F train ran back and forth
sometimes you could feel everything vibrate, just a little
and there was always at least a bit of noise
   coming from Queens Boulevard
and there was always at least a bit of a glow from
   the cars and streetlights
and when I went to bed each night
the lights from the headlights of the cars
would seep through the venetian blinds
and move across the ceiling
I liked to watch them dance at night
as I drifted off to sleep
my father worked in an automobile body shop
in the nearby neighborhood of Jamaica
he had never finished high school
back in the old country
back in the nineteen twenties
it didn't matter so much
and my father just wasn't the type for studying
he didn't have the patience for books
but he loved cars
and he knew everything about them
he wanted to design them
but he could only find work repairing and restoring them
his coworkers called him an artist
and why not?

his art was upholstery, body work
and paint
and he was frustrated because he knew more about cars
than his boss
but he made a living
and took care of his family
in this foreign land that became his home
and that's what really mattered
and we didn't have much
but I never felt deprived
some more toys would have been nice
like those GI Joes I wanted so much
but I knew I couldn't have everything I saw on TV
and I was happy playing with little knickknacks
I always had my imagination, anyway
and my father said that we couldn't afford very many toys, but
if I ever wanted a book, he would buy it for me
I could have all the books that I wanted
and as it turned out, I loved to read
I read everything I could get my hands on
I loved books
dearly, dearly, dearly
and he bought them for me
and I can't remember if I ever said
thank you daddy

Just Me

an only child
that's what they called me
no brothers
no sisters
and to this day
I cannot say
that I really understand
sibling rivalry or
sibling love
being an only child
meant that numbers were never on my side
only a child
in a world of adults
adjusting and adapting
feeling my way through
searching for my place
and if need be, putting on the mask of an adult
only an actor
performing on their stage
the undisputed star of their show
but it was lonely
at the top

World's Fair

some of my fondest memories from childhood
come from the New York World's Fair
nineteen sixty-four, sixty-five
it was practically in my backyard
well, maybe not quite so close
more like a few miles away, but visible
in the distance, from our apartment window
at night you could see the lights, and the fireworks
and we went there more times than I could count
and it was overwhelming, really too much to take in
through the eyes of a six- and seven-year-old
but I remember the monorail, and the trams
the moving sidewalks, rides and exhibits
the gadgets and inventions
the space age materials and nuclear energy
the robots and rockets, and there were dinosaurs too
the images of new cities, improbable products of
  architectural imagination
and a full scale, detailed model of New York City
the videophones, so crowded I never got to try them out
the ferris wheel that looked like a gigantic car tire
and dancing fountains, lit up by colored lights at night
the Hall of Science (one of my favorites)
the Carousel of Progress, and It's a Small World (which I adored)
the New York Exhibit (later featured in the movie Men in Black)
it consisted of two towers looking all futuristic and sci-fi
you could take an elevator up to the observation deck
to see the Manhattan skyline off in the distance
and then there was the Unisphere, the great symbol of the Fair
a globe ringed by satellites, representing the dream
of one world, at peace with itself
and there were exhibits from all the nations
and food from all over the world
but what I recall is being introduced to
foot long hot dogs
and most of all I remember that everyone was happy there
everyone was smiling and laughing
all of the people were so excited, thrilled, enthralled

and we were oh so very optimistic about the future
about progress, about tomorrow
it was before things got ugly
with Vietnam, and Watergate, and the oil shortage,
    and the hostage crisis
and everyone became cynical, and ironic
at the World's Fair, there was innocence, and faith
and promises of marvels soon to come
just like they promised us on TV and in the movies
promising us the world of The Jetsons, and Star Trek
and Kubrick's 2001
and we believed in it
I believed in it! I believed!
but it never came to be
promises unfulfilled
and when the World's Fair was over
they took most of it away
and the rest fell into disrepair
and the future, as it turns out
is history

Good Soldier

seventeen days after I was born
the Soviets launched Sputnik into orbit
its single beep, repeated over and over
chilled the heart of every man, woman, and child
in the free world
but not us newborns, no not us
we cried, but we were not afraid
when I was in elementary school
I was one of ten children chosen
to skip from second grade to fourth grade
there was a big push back then, you see
to accelerate our schooling
with special emphasis on science and mathematics
because the United States was in the midst of the Cold War
and we children were needed
because knowledge is power
because education is victory
because schools are the solution to every problem in America
I was tall for my age, so that part wasn't so bad
and the schoolwork wasn't a problem
but it was difficult being a year younger than most
almost two years younger than some
it was especially hard
because I was always a shy kid
socially awkward
it was painful at times
yes, at times
and at times
it was tough going
but maybe you noticed
how the Soviet Union isn't around anymore?
you're welcome!

When I Was Nine

my father died
when I was nine
following a lingering illness
cancer
they didn't tell me he was dying
wanted to shield me from it
maybe didn't know how to tell me
I don't know
I didn't know
I should have known
I didn't see
I saw the signs
I didn't understand
I should have understood
it's just that I thought
it's just that once upon a time I was told
that when you got sick
and went to the doctor
and went to the hospital
they would cure you
and you'd get better
and you'd go home
that's what I thought...
Surprise!
no, no, no
I don't mean to sound sarcastic or cynical
to be bitter or angry
though those feelings were no stranger to me
but no, no, no
really it's okay
that's life
it's just that it hurt
but it's all right
it was a long, long time ago
many many years
it still hurts
but it's okay
these things happen

much worse things happen to people
much worse...
so, it's all right
and no, no, no
I don't really want to talk about it anymore
except to say that
when I was nine
I learned that life is sadness
punctuated by moments of happiness
and the rest of the time
you just have to carry on
smiling through the tears
because that's life
and that's all I want to say about it
that's all

Fail-Safe

they sent us home from kindergarten
during the Cuban missile crisis
they didn't tell us why
I had no idea there was anything wrong
I was just happy to go home and play
in elementary school we had three kinds of drills
the fire drill where we went outside
breathing the air of normalcy
it was good to be out in the air
another drill where we lined up in the hallway
away from all of the windows
that was kind of fun
and a third drill where we went underneath our desks
that was the most fun of all
that was my favorite
and if those two drills had names
I don't recall them
they certainly weren't called
A-bomb drills or
H-bomb drills
and every weekday at noon
the air raid siren would go off
just testing
you could set your watch by it
and that was normal
just the way things were
that's all
it never felt like we were at war
but every apartment building in the neighborhood
that had a basement
also had a sign outside
that said, Fallout Shelter
my building didn't have a basement
that bothered me a little
black and white pictures and film
of mushroom clouds
were a familiar site on TV
in books, and in magazines
when they opened the Indian Point Nuclear Reactor
just north of New York City

we took a family trip up there to see it
they had guided tours
and later we had a class trip there as well
happy atoms
atoms for peace
by the time I was in fifth grade
we knew all about the bomb
and what it could do
what it could do to us
when I was a little bit older
I had one of those Time-Life educational books
it had a diagram showing how much would be destroyed
if an A-bomb and an H-bomb were dropped
on the Empire State Building
if it was an A-bomb
it looked like we'd be okay
where we lived in Queens
at least until the fallout
if it was an H-bomb
it didn't look so good
when I was ten
they showed the movie Fail-Safe on TV
and it ended with the bomb being dropped on New York City
they showed scenes of ordinary life
on the streets of the city
familiar images, to me
and then one by one they froze
and then the screen went to black
and despite the disclaimer that followed
saying this could never actually happen
I started screaming inside
I shouldn't have watched that movie that night
I really shouldn't have watched that movie
I couldn't sleep
I had trouble going to sleep for a long time
and for a couple of years afterwards
whenever I saw a plane overhead
I had shivers, I had chills, I was frightened
how silly, how silly, to be scared
of airplanes in the sky
flying over the city

how silly, how silly it was
a childish fear
especially considering that bombers carrying nuclear weapons
had long since been replaced
by Inter-Continental Ballistic Missiles
and the skies overhead were full of planes
passenger planes, nothing to be scared of
we were only a few miles from
John F. Kennedy Airport
and only a few miles from
LaGuardia Airport
and the rumbling of the jets was commonplace
when I was younger
and we had relatives flying into New York
we would go out to the airport to meet them
and back then the airport seemed like a special, magical place
that you would go to visit, just to see it
and we would go out onto the observation deck
to watch the airplanes
and they had binoculars
the kind you had to put a coin in
and they had gumball machines
but instead of candy, you'd get coins from other countries
my parents never flew in a plane
they came to this country on the Queen Elizabeth
I never flew in a plane
until I was twenty, and by then all the magic was gone
Fail-Safe was shown with commercial interruptions
and one of the sponsors was Salem cigarettes
this was before they banned cigarette ads from the air
from the air
and Salem had a jingle that went like this:
you can take Salem out of the country but
you can't take the country out of Salem
it had been repeated for years
everyone knew it by heart
but their newer commercials only played the first line
You can take Salem out of the country but...
ending abruptly
and then a little bell would ring
signaling viewers to complete the jingle on their own
from memory

which they did automatically
having learned it through years of repetition
you can take Salem out of the country but...
that half-jingle with its abrupt ending
was played during each commercial break of the movie
over and over and over again
and like Pavlov's dogs, I gained a conditioned response
only it was nausea, not salivation
and fear, not hunger
and it was my screen going to black
so that in the months that followed
whenever I heard that jingle
you can take Salem out of the country but...
I had shivers, chills, and frights
I hated that jingle, and they played it
over and over and over again
you can take Salem out of the country but...
thank God they got those commercials off the air
as I grew up, the fears faded away
but I still found airplanes strange, fearsome, and awe-inspiring
miraculous how these enormous machines
could just hang in the sky
seemingly suspended in midair
and as I grew up, while the fears faded away
sometimes
I still had nuclear nightmares
and it wasn't until much, much later
that it occurred to me that part of what was disturbing me
wasn't the death and the destruction alone
but the fact that it was always my hometown
that was being wiped out
in science fiction and disaster films
I was in Edgewater, New Jersey
looking across the Hudson River
at the Manhattan skyline
the Empire State Building
the Chrysler Building
and then I looked at the enormous black stain
rising up from the south of the island
in the autumn of 2001
and I wasn't afraid to die

no, I had gotten over that a long, long time ago
but I was afraid for my children
and for my hometown
and I wiped my eyes
and looked back at the skyline
and wondered
how long?
how long until

Reading Comics

a confession
I read comics, and
I was reading comics
since before I could read
I made my parents read them to me
they were relieved when I finally learned
how to read them for myself
comics were frowned upon in those days
the lowest of the low, it seemed
as art, and
as literature
but I read plenty of books
and I did well in school
so no one could say that comics
were rotting my brain
and I knew what I liked
I liked comics
newspaper funnies were good
but I loved the comic books the best
when I first started reading them
they were twelve cents a piece
and the annuals were a quarter
but unscrupulous merchants
decided to charge a penny tax
until the law cracked down
and justice was restored
I loved the superheroes most of all
Superman and Batman
the Flash and Green Lantern
Wonder Woman, and all the rest
and the Justice League of America
especially when they would team up
with the Justice Society of America
from another earth
later I discovered Marvel Comics
the Fantastic Four, the Incredible Hulk
Captain America, and the Avengers
and good old Spider-Man who came from Forest Hills
the neighborhood right next to my own

we had a lot in common, except for the spider-powers
he was a smart kid, picked on by bullies, not very popular
and he was being raised by his Aunt May
his Uncle Ben having died tragically
at the hands of a criminal
my father's name was Ben
you know, my four-colored friends
got me through some hard times growing up
there was so much to relate to
leaving behind an old world that was in the midst
   of self-destruction
delivered like the baby Moses to the safety of a new world
seeing your family murdered right in front of your eyes
and vowing, never again, never again
changing your name, putting on a disguise
hiding your identity, trying to fit in with everyone else
not letting them know who you really are or what
   you really can do
dedicating yourself to the cause of justice
like the Prophets of old
setting aside your own needs and wants
because other people need your help
protecting others, standing up for them
like the Judges of old
these were heroes created by people like me
although I didn't know it back then
they were the product
of the imagination
of young writers from immigrant families
writing stories of American heroes
writing from what they knew
those writers were the epic poets of our time
the true sons of Homer
but all I knew was that these heroes brought me comfort
and inspired me
and although it was a disappointment to finally realize
that I was never going to gain any superpowers
and that I could never put on a mask and cape
and go fight crime
I figured out that there are many different kinds of heroes
in this world
that it's a journey open to all of us

but I learned to keep my comic book reading to myself
most people just didn't understand
and I strayed away from my comic books a few times
   over the years
But I always returned to those ageless crusaders
those men and women of mystery
who strived to do what was right
without concern for reward or credit
and no matter the cost to themselves
but there came a time when collectors appeared
buying comics, bagging them
and not even reading them
just an investment, they thought
but the collectors came and went
and the heroes are still here
the heroes prevailed
and there came a time when new writers came along
hostile, thinking themselves bigger than the heroes
and wanting to make their mark
deconstructing the heroes
debasing them
even destroying them
and so, the heroes died
but in comics, no one dies forever
everyone comes back
everyone
and the writers may win for a time
but they don't own the heroes
the heroes are a part of us all
the heroes were there before those writers were born
and the heroes will be there after those writers are gone
and the heroes will win in the end
and good shall triumph over evil
and justice shall well up as waters
and righteousness as a mighty stream
so let there be heroes
and let them be us

Pizza by the Slice

pizza is my kryptonite
my weakness
my Achilles' heel
and nothing but nothing compares
to New York City pizza by the slice
pizza places were everywhere when I was growing up
like Danny's House of Pizza on Lefferts Boulevard
and Lydia's on Metropolitan Avenue
and Bus Stop Pizza which was on my block
over on Kew Gardens Road
right by the bus to Kennedy Airport
and the Union Turnpike subway station
and every few blocks you could find one
find a pizza place
so you never had to feel deprived
and you could sit on a stool to eat your slice
or order it through the window from the outside
and eat it on the go
folded in two, lengthwise
that's how we ate our slices
ate them in a rush
ate them on the run
when I was a kid
I used to watch the pizza men make the pies
starting with the dough, rolling it with a pin
twirling it around and around
sending it up in the air, and down again
I watched, and I went
wow
then they would ladle the sauce, add the mozzarella
and slide them into the oven
no toppings, no one asked for toppings in those days
no fancy stuff like today
just plain old pizza pie
pizza by the slice
they'd take the pie out of the oven
grab the pizza cutter
and cut the pie in half once
then twice
then twice more

eight slices to a pie
not six
not ten
eight
twenty-five cents for a slice
that's two bits, you know
as in, two pieces of eight
two bits of the old gold coin
the old Spanish dollar
eight slices in a pie
eight pieces in a gold coin
eight bits in a byte
pizza was my digital medium
my finger food
my most delicious computation
and I've been to some of the best restaurants, you know
I've eaten food from all over the world
I've been feted like a king on occasion
but none of it compares to the manna of my youth
New York City pizza
pizza by the slice
every day
after school
one kid I knew had a slice every hour on the hour
you could set your watch by him
and now that I've grown up
and grown out, out, out, out
I know that it's bad
I know that I need to lose weight
I know that it doesn't always agree with me
I know that I shouldn't
but
slices of pizza are like chunks of my home planet
that render me powerless
weak
and unable to resist
oh well...
another slice please, Bizarro

That I Am

In the space between words

In the space between breaths

In the space between thoughts

I am

Acknowledgements

Several poems in this anthology were previously published in varying forms: "Sand," "Soap," and "That I Am" were published in *Anekaant*; "Memorial Day 2009" in ETC; "Head First" in *Poetica*; "My Ana Marred," "Inundations," "Ghetto," and "Five Windows" in *Samyutka*; and "The Ten Commandments" in the *General Semantics Bulletin* as part of an article entitled, "The Ten Commandments and the Semantic Environment: Understanding the Decalogue Through General Semantics and Media Ecology," which was later included in my book, *On the Binding Biases of Time and Other Essays on General Semantics and Media Ecology* (Institute of General Semantics, 2011).

I am thankful for the opportunity to publish this poetry collection, and would like to begin by expressing my gratitude to my friends at NeoPoiesis Press, especially the press's peerless leader Dale Winslow. Also, the estimable Stephen Roxborough. Many of the poems collected here originated within the context of the old MySpace poetry community, from which I drew inspiration and instruction, and I would like to single out the late Si Philbrook as especially influential. And from MySpace to real space, I am grateful to Robert Priest for his friendship and guidance.

I have dedicated this volume to Adas Emuno, and from that spiritual community I want to thank Barry Schwartz, Iris Karlin, Joe Flaxman, Elka Oliver, Sandy Horowitz, Kerith Shapiro, and everyone in our Poetry Garden group, especially Doris White, Lauren Rowland, Linda Kowalski, and Norm Rosen. Thinking back on my youth, I would also like to acknowledge Temple Isaiah of Forest Hills, and from that congregation Jacob Polish, Boris Voronovsky, Stephen Pearce, Bob Ourach, and Steve Sher. And my youthful companions, the group including Marty Friedman, Robert Ossias, and Keith Newman, still at their peak, no matter the years.

I am grateful as well to many many friends and colleagues, so many more than I can recall, but some who immediately come to mind are Thom Gencarelli, Mike Plugh, Eva Berger, Terry Manzella, Corey Anton, Adeena Karasick, Lillian Allen, Teri McLuhan, Karen Michelle Johnston, Marleen Barr, Paul Levinson, Joshua Meyrowitz, Gary

Gumpert, Susan Drucker, Nora Bateson, Stephen Nachmanovitch, Elena Lamberti, as well as Christine Nystrom and Neil Postman.

Finally, my family is intimately bound up in this collection, and in everything I do, including my wife Barbara, my son Benjamin, my daughter Sarah, and my parents of blessed memory, Betty and Benjamin Strate.

About the Author

Lance Strate is the author of 10 books, including 2 other books of poetry, *Thunder at Darwin Station* (2015), and *Diatribal Writes of Passage in a World of Wintertextuality* (2020), as well as *On the Binding Biases of Time* (2011), *Amazing Ourselves to Death* (2014), *Media Ecology* (2017), and *Concerning Communication* (2022). He is co-editor of 7 additional books, including a poetry collection entitled *The Medium is the Muse* (2014), as well as 2 editions of *Communication and Cyberspace* (1996, 2003), *The Legacy of McLuhan* (2005), *Korzybski And...* (2012), and *Taking Up McLuhan's Cause* (2017). His poetry has been published in *New Note Poetry*, *Poetica*, *Anekaant*, *Samyutka*, *KronoScope*, *ETC*, *Explorations in Media Ecology*, *General Semantics Bulletin*, on the *Malahat Review* website, and in several anthologies, and he is also the author of 5 Purim spiel musicals, a script for the children's animated television series *Galaxy Rangers*, and approximately 300 articles and essays. Translations of his writing have appeared in French, Spanish, Italian, Portuguese, Hungarian, Hebrew, Mandarin, and Quenya, and several of his poems have been set to music.

He currently holds the title of Professor of Communication and Media Studies at Fordham University. He is also President of the Institute of General Semantics, and is a past president and board member of the New York Society for General Semantics, the New York State Communication Association, and the Media Ecology Association, as well as the Senior Vice-President of the Global Listening Centre. Dr. Strate held the 2015 Harron Family Chair in Communication at Villanova University, and received an honorary appointment as Chair Professor in the School of Journalism and Communication at Henan University in Kaifeng, China, in 2016.

Lance Strate served as President of Congregation Adas Emuno, a Reform synagogue in Bergen County, New Jersey, for 6 years, and is a member of the temple's Board of Trustees. On occasion, he serves as lay leader for Friday evening Shabbat services, and delivers sermons that are sometimes said to be thought-provoking.

Printed in the USA
CPSIA information can be obtained
at www.ICGtesting.com
LVHW092047030124
767895LV00014B/725